Parachute
Action Adventure

for Kids

By

LIONEL PAXTON

CONTENTS

Introduction

Man first had an idea about parachutes hundreds of years ago. Since then, the shape of the parachute has been changed a number of times to become the parachute we see used today. The modern parachute is much easier to steer and turn than the original invention.

In the 18th century Benjamin Franklin was the first person to come up with the idea of a lot of soldiers using parachutes to jump out of a plane to fight the enemy. In the First World War, soldiers using parachutes were called paratroopers. Today, almost every country in the world has paratroopers trained and ready to jump out of airplanes.

Being a paratrooper is a thrilling and exciting job with lots of adventure and possible danger for both men and women. You have to learn to skydive and to be a soldier. Jumping out of an airplane can be a lot of fun but it becomes dangerous when you are going where the enemy is.

---oooOOOooo---

"A mind is like a parachute. It doesn't work if it is not open."
- Frank Zapper

This quote was often used by Frank Zapper, an American musician, composer, guitarist, recording engineer, record producer, and film, director. Rolling Stone magazine ranked him 71st on its list of the "100 Greatest Artists of All Time".

Sir James Dewar, who is the original author of this quote, states that your mind should be open to learning, the way a parachute has to open to work.

Parachute Action Adventure

What is a parachute and how does it work?

A parachute is a large piece of fabric that opens out and captures the air. The first parachutes were made from silk that was light and could be packed into a small area.

Today parachutes are made from nylon which is specially woven with extra thick thread to make it strong enough for the huge pressures of wind against it, and this can be easily seen by the pattern of small squares it creates.

Nylon has been chosen as the best fabric because it can stretch like elastic, it is not affected by mildew or mold, it is easy to get and most of all it costs a lot less than silk. The harness and the straps (called suspension lines) which link you to the parachute are all made of nylon as well.

When the parachute opens, this is called deploying; you will feel a sudden pull upwards for about 10 seconds before you start to go down toward the ground again.

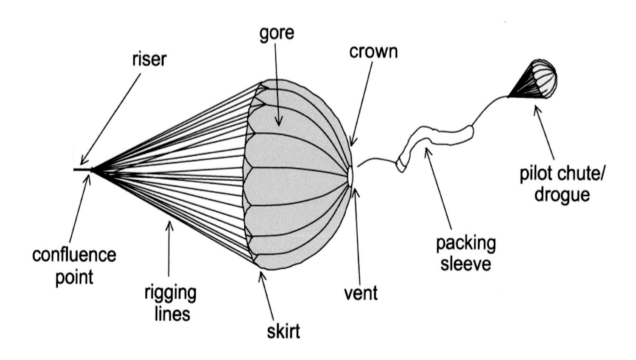

Types of parachutes

Today, there are lots of different types of parachutes used, but skydivers and paratroopers really only use 2 main types:

- **Round**

  This parachute is often used when cargo is dropped to the ground from aircraft. These parachutes open automatically as the cargo leaves the plane. They are used by the army to land equipment that includes vehicles for the paratroopers to use.

These parachutes look like large round jellyfish as they drop the ground. They cannot be steered and turned unless they have been changed before a jump. These parachutes are rarely used by paratroopers and skydivers these days.

- **Square**

  These are the modern parachutes that you will have seen used by skydivers and paratroopers. They open out into a square or a rectangular shape when the cord is pulled. These parachutes are very easy to steer and turn.

A skilled person can land on a marked spot on the ground which is a long way from the point where they jump out of the airplane.

Square parachutes slow a person down a lot more than the round parachute, so they can have a safer landing. Today, the US Army uses a parachute that will slow down the drop from 21 feet per second to 15 feet per second. This makes it a lot safer for a paratrooper.

The other parachute types are Ram-Air, Ribbon and Ring. These are specialist types of parachute for special needs.

- **Ram-air**

  This type of parachute opens up on its own without the cord being pulled. They give better control over direction and speed.

- **Ribbon and ring**

  Here are parachutes that are designed for very quick speeds and where a lot of strength in needed. These types of parachutes often have a hole in the middle to reduce the pressure on the fabric and to stop the parachute from tearing as it goes down.

History

Parachutes have been used for hundreds of years. History shows them being used in China in the 1100s. About 1495, the famous painter, Leonardo da Vinci, designed a pyramid-shaped parachute with a wooden frame, but he probably never tested his idea. Then in 2000, a daredevil called Adrian Nichols built a parachute based on Leonardo's drawings and found that the parachute worked when he used it.

In 1784, American founding father Benjamin Franklin spoke about using airborne soldiers. He thought this would be a good way to get soldiers into enemy country before anyone knew they were there. As a visionary he could see not only parachutes in the future but also airborne troops parachuting into battle, but this didn't happen for another couple of hundred years.

This idea of an airborne force has been used ever since the First World War in 1918, when soldiers jumped from planes to land behind the enemy lines. Ever since then, paratroopers have been used in almost every war.

When soldiers jump behind enemy lines, this is now called a 'parachute drop'. The first time the phrase 'parachute drop' was used was in 1927 by the Italian army.

Paratroopers were used a lot in the Second World War; in fact they were often used as regular soldiers at times when there were not enough soldiers on the ground.

After the end of the Second World War in 1945, there were lots of parachutes left over and lots of former soldiers who wanted to jump out of planes for fun. This started the hobby and sport of parachuting. Lots of people joined this new sport and competitions started.

In the 1950s, a man called Raymond Young had an idea of 'skydiving' and he opened up a skydiving center, where people paid money to skydive. This became a popular sport and in 1957 lots of sky diving schools were opened.

In 1967, the United States Parachute Association (USPA) was started. This club began in 1930 and was called the National Parachute Riggers-Jumpers Inc. It then changed its name to the Parachute Club of America. (PCA), and then finally became the United States Parachute Association.

Paratroopers and skydiving heroes

Paratroopers and skydivers have a very thrilling and sometimes dangerous life. They often need to be heroic when taking part in sporting events or when in dangerous places.

We see them in movies as the good guys and the bad guys but we don't often see them pictured in modern photographs about war until they are on the ground where they look like any other soldier in combat. It is only in movies and television shows that we see paratroopers jumping out of planes and maneuvering a parachute to land. It is how they get to be in combat that makes them different from other soldiers.

They don't arrive in a boat, like in the Navy or land in an airplane like in the Air Force or arrive in trucks like in the Army. Paratroopers arrive in airplanes but they all jump out before the plane lands. They will often jump out of the plane at night, so the enemy can't see them.

A paratrooper uses a parachute like a sky diver does. He has to be trained in sky diving and how to use the parachute before he can become a paratrooper.

Skydiving is an action sport where people jump from an airplane and use a parachute to slow them down until they land back on the ground.

Before you make your first jump, you will be given some basic training and important instructions about how to and when to leave the plane, free falling and then pulling the cord on your parachute, and finally how to land correctly without injuring yourself.

The thrill from skydiving comes from jumping out of a very good airplane that there is no reason to leave apart from the excitement as you jump. Your heart will be beating fast and you will probably be very scared the first time.

The free fall part of the jump is before you use your parachute. You fall very fast towards the ground and then open your parachute to slow you down and help you steer and turn to the landing point.

Each time you jump you will feel the same rush of excitement and the fear will disappear as you realize that you will land safely on the ground. To be a paratrooper you have to be able to skydive first and really like jumping from a plane. Not everybody can do this. Some people are just too scared to even try.

13

What is a paratrooper?

A paratrooper is a specially trained soldier who jumps out of an airplane into enemy territory or into an area that is hard to get to by foot or in a vehicle. They have trained to be a skydiver and then need extra skills to be a paratrooper.

They are intelligent and able to plan ahead and are very well trained in fighting and armed combat. They become self-confident in their abilities and of those of their team.

Who can be a paratrooper?

Any person in the Armed Forces can apply to be part of the Airborne Forces. The Airborne Forces is the department that tests and trains people to see if they can become a paratrooper.

If you wanted to become a paratrooper, the first thing you would have to do is army training. Once you had completed this, you would go to a school where they would teach you how to use a parachute and test you to make sure you were able to do the job. Lots of people start the training, but fail the tests and are unable to become a paratrooper. You can only become a paratrooper once you have finished all the training and passed all the tests.

Physical fitness

Paratroopers are strong and very fit. As part of the training, a person wanting to be a paratrooper has to do a lot of physical challenges, this is to make sure that they are fit enough to jump from a plane wearing a parachute.

There is a lot of work which can be done to help you get fit. This would involve learning some skills on how to fight and survive, as well as training your brain and getting your body fit.

Physical training

Paratroopers are expected to meet high standards of physical fitness and the training is extremely structured and intense. You will have to pass a physical fitness test before any training.

Physical training starts on the ground teaching the skills that helps you to make a safe parachute jump, without hurting yourself when landing. You will train with an artificial door to get used to exiting an airborne aircraft, as well as jump landing onto a platform to learn the correct parachute landing skills.

Also, you will practice controlling your parachute during a descent on a lateral drift device. Then you will advance to leaping from a 34-foot tower to rehearse the actual feeling of a parachute jump.

Your training will progress with more intensity. You will learn how to deal with swinging and swaying falls when landing, and how to handle being dragged. You will progress to jump from a scary 250-foot tower to further rehearse the actual parachute jump.

You will be trained how to leave the aircraft safely, deploy your parachute and to land safely on the ground. All of this is done over and over again until the instructor says you are ready to fly in the plane and jump.

After about 3 weeks you will finally jump from an aircraft where you will have to make 5 qualifying jumps, using both ordinary round parachutes and steerable square parachutes.

That is when the magic starts to happen, the electrifying view of the earth from 2 miles up and the feeling of flying, the plane disappearing above you, and the thrill of the parachute ride.   Then it's time to do more.

Advanced physical training techniques teach them to do things like jump into water in diving gear.   Very advanced and very dangerous!

Safe landing

The correct landing technique with a parachute is practiced by paratroopers and skydivers. It allows a parachutist to land safely and without injury. The feet strike the ground first and, immediately the parachutist throws himself sideways to distribute the shock of landing through the body when hitting the ground.

During landing the parachutist's legs are slightly bent at the knee, the chin is tucked in, and the parachute risers are usually held in an arm-bar protecting the face and throat. The elbows are tucked into the sides to prevent injury. Some parachutists prefer to land with their hands linked behind the neck with elbows tucked in close.

When landing the body should contact the ground along 5 points in this order:

- balls of the feet
- side of the calf
- side of the thigh
- side of the hip, or buttocks
- side of the back on the muscle.

With repeated practice parachutists learn to make smooth falls automatically that becomes a reflex action. Experienced jumpers are able land in a standing or a running position at a low landing speed, and remain upright on arriving at the landing site.

Being a paratrooper

Life as a paratrooper is living as part of an elite hard hitting combat team that use planes and helicopters to place them in or near the battle ground.

There is support from ground troops and other units taking part in the combat.

You need to like some adventurous activities as you will be placed in different situations and locations around the world. You need to enjoy:

- Being a risk taker and getting the adrenalin rush
- Working and doing activities outdoors
- Flying or being in different aircraft
- Target and game shooting
- Driving different vehicles
- Going into conflict and daring situations.

You need to be interested in various activities and have experience in lots of different fields, including:

- Combat and armed combat
- Handling explosives and ammunition
- Vehicle and equipment maintenance
- Paramedic and first aid survival training
- Communication equipment.

As you can see being a paratrooper is a lot more than just jumping out of a plane for the excitement. It takes a lot of hard work to be a paratrooper. They are often the first people sent to an area to look around and to find out if other troops can get to the area safely.

Who can learn to skydive?

Both men and women can learn to skydive and enjoy the thrill of jumping out of an airplane and landing safely on the ground.

You need to be 18 years old so you are responsible to make your own decisions and strong enough to pull the parachute cord and safely land. You should be fit and active and not weigh more than 250 pounds.

Danger

Armed forces paratroopers are usually employed by the airborne divisions as highly specialized troops. They are required to meet very high standards of courage, intelligence, and physical fitness.

Being a paratrooper develops leadership skills, strong self-confidence, and a forceful spirit in really challenging physical and mental conditioning.

Being a paratrooper looks thrilling and lots of fun but it is a dangerous job that is only for brave soldiers who like to take risks. You need to be a good soldier first and then learn how to skydive and get into enemy territory.

Skydiving soldiers can easily penetrate battlefields behind the enemy lines, because they can be dropped from the sky. They can also spy on enemy territory, or provide necessary backup in areas which are hard to reach by land quickly.

Paratroopers need to know first aid in case any of them get hurt while landing or afterwards. There is often no one else around who can help them.

Parachute Action Adventure

Many people like to romanticize this glamorous military position which is quite dangerous when facing the real and dangerous business of fighting the enemy.

However, even as a civilian skydiver, landing on the ground while descending under a parachute can be somewhat dangerous, particularly if landing in a tree, shallow water, a road with racing traffic, or being blown into tall building!

Parachute trivia

The very first parachute was made from linen in China during the early 1100s, however silk was soon adopted because of its light weight, strength, easy to pack, fire resistant, and springy.

In addition to the fabric canopy, a parachute is equipped with a harness that is worn by the jumper. Attached to the harness is a back-pack that holds the canopy; often a jump-suit is worn together with boots, helmet, goggles, gloves and altimeter to judge the height for pulling the ripcord to open the chute.

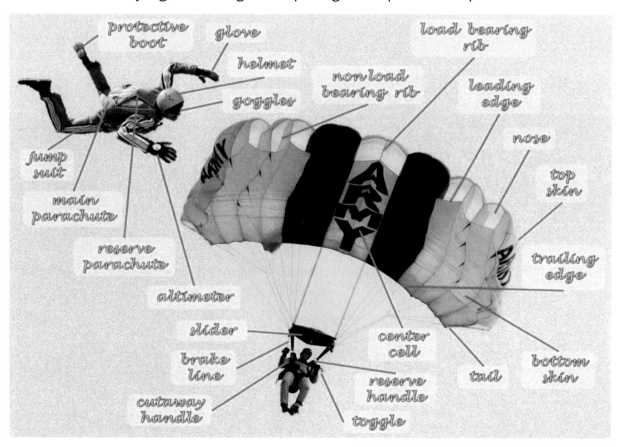

A parachute is a lift creating or wind resistance device made of fabric. They can be used to allow its wearer to jump, or skydive, from an aircraft or fixed object and land safely. They are also used to slow aircraft, motor vehicle or spacecraft.

Fatality rate in the United States is measured to be around 1 in 80,000 jumps.

Safety requirements ensure parachutes are carefully folded and packed to assure that it opens reliably. Emergency parachutes, usually called the reserve chute, are packed by specially trained riggers who must be certified according to legal standards.

Failure to open it is usually caused by the "streamer" and in most cases the lines are twisted preventing the canopy to open enough do to catch the air. Jumpers usually try to open a streamer by shaking the lines. If this fails, they open their emergency parachute.

About 1 in a 100 parachutes fail to open due to a streamer failing and emergency parachutes the incidence improves to about 1 in 500 parachutes failing to open.

Roger Moore skiing off a cliff pulling a union jack parachute in the film The Spy Who Loved Me, the world of James Bond 007, full of action, excitement, drama and danger. The stunt man playing the part almost hit something in mid-air... a lucky escape from a camera.

Orange and White Parachute features in the film Goldfinger climaxing with Bond and Goldfinger fighting to the death. A gunshot decompresses the plane and Goldfinger is sucked out of the jet. With the jet in a nosedive, plummeting towards the sea, Bond and Pussy Galore leap to safety using the parachute. On the ground the escape item proves useful, concealing their passionate embrace from potential rescuers.

During World War II, the United States was unable to import silk from Japan, so parachute manufacturers instigated using nylon fabric for parachute canopies which turned out to be superior to silk as it was more elastic, better resistant to mildew, and much less expensive. Supplementary fabrics like Dacron and Kevlar in recent times have been used, but nylon remains the best material.

Parachute fabricators are continually searching for better materials and designs whereby the most intriguing future development is the potential use to control the emergency descent of entire aircraft. For example, Ballistic Recovery Systems Inc. (BRS), is already manufacturing such General Aviation Recovery Devices (GARDs) for use on small airplanes.

Development of parachutes really began in the eighteenth century and Andre Jacques Garnerin made numerous parachute jumps from hot air balloons, first jumping in 1797, in Paris from an altitude of 2,000 feet (600 meters).

The backpack parachute design was invented in 1911, comprising the ripcord, a quick release mechanism which allowed jumpers to control the exact moment of releasing the parachute.

Thief DB Cooper jumped with 2 parachutes from a Boeing 727 at 10,000 feet going 170 miles per hour with 200,000 USD on November 24, 1971. He was the only recorded case of skyjacker on USA territory that has escaped capture by the FBI. His landing area pinpointed to Lake Merwin, he's never been found.

In 1944 during World War II the largest airborne operation was mounted where over 20,000 soldiers parachuted in close proximity of Arnhem in Holland to seize a vital bridge from the Germans which would provide a rapid advance of British and American mechanized forces into Northern Germany. The operation failed as a result of strong German resistance and intervention of bad weather.

Depicted is the catalog of necessities for the Parachute Brigade typical soldiers' kit inventory for war, Battle of Arnhem.

An American strategic bluff was instituted by the creation of Special Phantom Airborne Divisions during World War II where these official US Army Airborne Divisions existed only on paper, but had recruits wear insignias around and in towns with the objective of convincing the spies in England that the Americans had more trained Airborne Divisions than they really had... It worked and the ghosts did their bluff.

6th Airborne Division   9th Airborne Division   18th Airborne Division   21st Airborne Division   135th Airborne Division

World War II Special Phantom Airborne Divisions

Largest formation of Skydivers took the world record in February 2004, in Takhli Thailand, with a 357-way grouping which flew for exactly 6 seconds before breaking up.

The highest altitude record from which a parachute jump was performed by Joseph Kittinger in August 1960, jumping from an open gondola carried aloft by large helium balloon at altitude of 101,516 feet (30,942 m) and experiencing temperatures as low as −94 °F (−70 °C) during his descent and reaching a top speed of 614 mph (988 km/h).

Joseph Kittinger also in 1960 set a world record for the longest skydive from a height greater than 19 miles (31 kilometers).

Parachute Action Adventure

The lowest recorded Parachute jump was carried out by the German combat paratroopers known as the Fallschirmjager, who jumped from 250 feet into Crete during World War II.

Youngest person to Skydive leaps into the record books was 4 year-old Toni Stadler in a tandem parachute jump took place in Cape Town South Africa, strapped to jumpmaster Paul Lutge's chest as they leaped out of their single-engine plane 10,000 feet above the earth, freefalling for half a minute before opening the parachute.

Oldest woman to skydive was 90 year-old Marni Evans in February 2 2002, who literally dropped in for her 90th birthday party, jumping from an airplane at 12,000 feet.

Eldest solo jumper was 92 year-old Englishman Herb Tanner with artificial knees made it into the record books by becoming the oldest person ever to jump out of an airplane, leaping out at 3,500 feet.

And the oldest tandem jumper was set by Estrid Geertsen at 100 years old, back in October 1999, from an altitude of 13,100 feet (4,000 meters) over Roskilde Denmark.

The average age of sport skydivers is between 30-39 years old and 84% of them are males.

Military parachutes have a set service-life without use of 16.5 years, every parachute is stamped with a manufacturing date that starts its life-cycle clock. and also stamped with the date that it is first placed in service (PIS) from which a parachute's service life cannot exceed 12 years.

There are 306 parachute drop-zone centers worldwide, 54 in Canada and 252 in the US.

If you have enjoyed this ebook, **please** leave a helpful Customer Review on Amazon.

Digital Edition V 0.1 – Copyright 2013

---oooOOOooo---

Other Books by Author

Lionel Paxton is an author who has recently turned his hand to children's books. He saw the need for informative picture books for children from the age of 5 to 10. Books are typically the first exposure to learning and art that children get which urges one to make the very best books possible. He understands how important books were to his childhood. With them, he feels as if transported to some parallel universe, a world of grace and wonder.

Navy Seal Dogs by Lionel Paxton

☆☆☆☆☆

Formats

Kindle Edition

Paperback

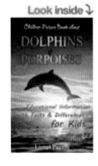

Dolphins and Porpoises Children Picture Book by Lionel Paxton

☆☆☆☆☆

Formats

Kindle Edition

Paperback

The Legend of the Stars by Lionel Paxton

☆☆☆☆☆

Formats

Kindle Edition

Paperback

---oooOOOooo---

Made in the USA
Las Vegas, NV
26 July 2021